# DIRECTING YOUR DEBUT

*How to HACK YOUR MINDSET to
DIRECT A BADASS FIRST FILM*

*(Short, Feature, or Anything in Between)*

(PART ONE)

Christopher Folkens

ISBN - 978-0-578-61256-0

# DEDICATION

This book is dedicated to all the young filmmakers out there that have the unrealized dream to direct their debut feature film. Now is your time.

# CONTENTS

## The *DIRECTING YOUR DEBUT* Resources

The FREE companion items to this book, including printable handouts and book updates are available at: www.directingyourdebut.com/book

Please access these items now before you forget.

For BOOKING INFO contact:
chris@directingyourdebut.com

# ACKNOWLEDGMENTS

FOR MY PARENTS: I am beyond grateful for all you have done to make life special through the years. You are loving, wise, trustworthy, compassionate, patient and empowering.

FOR MY AMAZING TEAM ON CATALYST: There are no words that express the gratitude for my entire team of amazing producers, cast, artisans and other crew members. This film would not have been possible without your dedication and commitment to excellence and Truth in your art. I acknowledge you for showing up and re-inventing every day. You all brought your A-game and it shows.

FOR MY MENTORS, TEACHERS, COACHES: I acknowledge you for the loving interruption you create in the world. You are winning the world to harmony and bringing us all back to who we really are. You are showing everyone that they truly matter and their contribution in life matters. You are an example of what it means to choose life instead of survival.

MUCH GRATITUDE to my editor Chiwan Choi at Writ Large Press. You've been a phenomenal source of wisdom and encouragement on this journey in writing this book.

# 1   **THE DREAM**

You've had a dream all your life.

You've had an idea for a film.

But nothing is happening.

Or worse yet? YOU are what's happening.
You're self-sabotaging your own path. You're letting
your own drama get in the way of telling your stories.

You may not want to let on that that's the case.
Why? Because in the world of the whole "red pill / blue

pill" *Matrix* style choice in front of you, that red pill is a tough pill to swallow. That choice to face the "truth" means we actually get to own the fact that the reason I'm not doing what I love is my own damn fault.

Now. I hesitate to use the term "fault" here because what I really mean is it is my own *responsibility*. "My own damn fault" just sounds better.

To be clear, I'm not some Pulitzer prize winning author.

In fact, I am not an "author." Yet. (So I'm going to use that as creative license to have fun with this book and "speak" candidly so beware of "F-bombs" and other colloquialisms.)

Once upon a time….

I wasn't a filmmaker either. But things changed. Because I TOOK ACTION. I stopped talking myself out of doing something. As a result, I'm creating the life I've always dreamed of living.

In much the same way, it was time to get my thoughts on this subject out on paper for all of you to read in such a way that will hopefully inspire YOU to take action toward the life of your dreams.

It all boils down to this: when you face, confront and break through the very real ways you are your own worst enemy, on the other side of that is one thing:

FREEDOM.

FREEDOM to LIVE your dream instead of just "having" a dream.

FREEDOM to follow your passions while learning to master the fear that inherently comes with going against the status quo or putting yourself out on the skinny branches.

FREEDOM to follow your inner intuition and learn to "trust the process" of life.

So how did I actually make the shift? Long story (hence why I'm writing a book). Ultimately, my *vision and commitments* became bigger than my stories about why I couldn't do it or why I shouldn't do it.

At the end of the day, I get what it's like to dream all your life about being a filmmaker. Wondering if it would ever happen. So, I'm simply sharing this in hopes that it inspires filmmakers around the world to go out and make films that leave a powerful mark on the world.

So this is my story.

A story of how I faced what was holding me back and found a way. I found a way even when life / God / the Universe wanted to test me at every turn. (Funny how that works right?) I'm grateful for the tests along the way, and yet, nevertheless, I believe the true test was whether I was willing to do whatever it took to elevate myself to the level where that film could be possible

At every turn, directing my debut feature film, *CATALYST,* has called me to new levels of leadership, personal effectiveness, commitment, and ultimate spiritual growth.

To give you a glimpse into the making of *CATALYST,* I set out to direct a feature film but I knew it was going to require an extremely non-traditional approach to getting it done.

I didn't have a complete script.

I didn't have a budget.

I didn't have funding.

I didn't have celebrities (yet).

I didn't have a team around me.

All I had was a dream.  It was a dream where my art would reflect the darkest parts of humanity in a way that would invite the audience to question their own beliefs, judgments, and fears. They would become a part of the journey of the characters by participating in the puzzle the film presents to the characters.

The vision was born.  But the mechanisms by which I would bring that vision to life were yet to be determined.

Throughout this book I'll attempt to showcase the various strategies it took to ultimately bring that vision to life.  But in order to fully grasp what we need to back way up and discuss the mindsets it took to FORGE a path where there was NO PATH.

There is no one right way to make a movie, but what I know will never change is that we all face fear. We all face our own internal ego conversations that like to keep us in a box. These ego conversations prevent everything from deep meaningful connections in our lives, all the way to truly preventing us from living a life worth living.

It is my stand that this book serves to be the ultimate interruption for you in your journey to become the filmmaker you were destined to be. I am standing for the notion that if you were called to begin reading this book and something about it resonates with you, you were destined to tell a story that is not only important *to you*, but *important to this world*.

The story that calls to you is calling YOU forth.

The story that calls to you, demands that you get out of your own way and CHOOSE to rise above your limitations. The story that calls to you, requires you to believe and have FAITH that you will overcome everything that is holding you back.

All of this will become reality when you choose to believe that YOU ARE ENOUGH. That is the platform from which we get to operate here. The hard truth is that because, in reality, you ARE enough, you are also exactly what is in your own way. How do I know this? RESULTS. You haven't taken action.

You're waiting.

…and waiting.

…and waiting.

However, instead of taking offense to that assertion, I invite you to choose to look at it from an empowering place. Because you only have to look in the mirror, that means you have the power to shift and therefore change the outcome of your life.

Am I talking about only filmmaking here?

Hell no.

In fact, change one area of your life and you will necessarily impact every other area of your life. They say, "How you do anything is how you do everything," and there is a ridiculous amount of truth to that statement.

Why? Because when you change how you THINK, you change how you DO. And when you change how you DO, you change your LIFE.

We will do a deep dive into this any many more concepts throughout this book. So buckle up!

## JUST FOR FILMMAKERS?

Hell no. Although there are an abundance of directing skills and tricks of the trade throughout this book, the ultimate focus of this book is on the mindset it took to do what I once considered "impossible."

If you are struggling in any domain of your life, you're likely in for a hell of a ride here too.

Why?

Because this book, serves as dramatic mirror for how you're living your life. When you start to realize all the ways you're getting in your own way, chances are you'll notice those aspects affect you in every aspect of your life.

The good news is that when you create a dynamic shift in one area of your life, it will necessarily impact other areas of your life as well because it is your underlying BELIEF structure that is running the show subconsciously.

But first, let's define our mission.


## DEFINING OUR MISSION

Chances are you picked up the book because 1.) you have a burning desire to direct (or pursue some creative endeavor that requires you to put you're ass on the line, skin in the game, and risk looking like a fool, 2.) you're intrigued by what I have to say, or 3.) you are out to somehow "prove me wrong" because you think you know better, or are just committed to "being right" about your own egocentric philosophy. If you're the latter, put the book down now, return it, whatever you do, DO NOT read the section of this book that is specifically devoted to "your kind."

For those of you who are left, welcome.

What follows here is a deep dive into the world of personal effectiveness and leadership skills that, when combined, fully supported me becoming the person I needed to be to rise above my circumstances, limiting beliefs, and external obstacles in order to achieve a lifelong mission => directing my feature debut film CATALYST.

You might be saying: *"It's awfully presumptuous to declare we're going to make a 'badass' feature film."* Well, I invite you to shoot for the moon, my dear friend. I personally believe there needs to be a sense of bold authenticity to whatever you create. The term "badass" isn't used here lightly, nor is it meant to be crass. The people I would consider "badass" in my life are the most unapologetically and uniquely themselves. They are masters of their craft. For instance, look up my friend Roy Elghanayan on YouTube. That man is a badass. He is a Krav Maga master like no other. His commitment to his craft is exceptional. That same commitment to mastery of craft is what I want for YOU. So just notice if your attachment to what the descriptor "badass" means could be blocking you from seeing all possibilities. If that is holding you back with a title, where else is that thought process (attachment) holding you back in life?

This book will hopefully serve as the catalyst for you to begin your path to overcome the internal obstacles that are holding you back.

I can be your guide on this journey, should you choose it. But it requires several essential "pre-requisites" before we go any further.

1) You need to be willing to DO THE WORK. This book isn't going to change you. My "Directing Your Debut" online course isn't going to change you. My coaching program isn't going to change you. All of these things are nothing but catalysts for change. YOU must be committed, face the difficult things in your life only you get to face, take committed action, and then EARN the results. The course, my coaching, this book, and every other program or platform in life will not work unless you actually get committed to something and fundamentally change your relationship with what "commitment" means. More on that later...

2) Be COACHABLE. You need to be open to

looking at things differently. YOUR 'winning' ways got you where you are. Now is your time to try something new. When I coach people I often use the phrase "your limitations got you here, now let's see what we can create when we bust through those limitations." Nothing will happen if your proverbial "cup" is already full. You must be willing to "unlearn what you have learned" in order to try on something new. Yes. You can call me Yoda from now on.

But again, nothing will happen unless you face your fears, confront what stops you, and choose a life of mastering what it is like to consistently break through that which holds you back from living that life worth living. For us, it just so happens that that "life worth living" statement means directing the films we are called to direct and that we are living our life's purpose.

Theodore Roosevelt once said *"Each time we face our fear, we gain strength, courage, and confidence in the doing."*

Now. Is. Your. Time.

## WHAT DOES BEING A FILMMAKER MEAN TO YOU?

The massively successful Hollywood producer Jerry Bruckheimer would always say about filmmakers that "We're in the transportation business. We transport audiences from one place to another."

Another WORLD. Another LIFE. Another EXPERIENCE.

For a brief window of time, the filmmaker yields the power to transport people into a shared experience where we live vicariously through the eyes of heroes and villains alike.

We transport people from one reality into another, temporarily relieving pain, struggle, heartache in some cases. In others, the filmmaker inspires or supports the audience in transcending their limitations and rising above oppressive forces. As we follow Luke Skywalker on his mythic "hero's journey," or fall in love all over again as we live vicariously through a silver screen romance, or perhaps we put our minds to the test in following along with the latest mind-bender from one of my favorite filmmakers, Christopher Nolan.

The thing that really resonates with me about being

a director is that the director has their finger on the pulse of all the different aspects of the storytelling process. The director is in position to enable and empower all the various artists to do their best work. The director stands to create synchronicity amongst all of the different disciplines that tell the story.

Everything we all do is in service of the story. What is at stake, or what is possible when this story is told?

Being a director mean standing as source, or cause, and coming from "ownership" at all times. This is a bit of an esoteric concept that may not make sense at first, but with time will hopefully resonate on a deep level with you.

I don't mean coming from "ownership" as if to say legal ownership. The director is not necessarily the one who came up with the kernel of the idea, first. Maybe you are, maybe you aren't, but it IS about being a servant to that greater story. Again, what is at stake thematically, or in the world, by the story you're telling? The director gets to be the guardian of that TRUTH. Protect it at all costs. I always say that I'm a servant to the story – not necessarily the script, because things get rewritten constantly – in pre-production, production, and post-production.

## WHAT STORY IS CALLING YOU?

What is that core essence that demands to be told? If you want to get esoteric with it, I think that there's something about the human experience that is always dying to be brought forth in the work of cinema.

In the brilliant book *"Big Magic: Creative Living Beyond Fear"* Elizabeth Gilbert refers to real world instances where creative ideas actually pop up for creative people around the world and if they don't follow it, those ideas actually may end up going to someone else who WILL follow it, almost as if transferring from one person to another in the collective consciousness. It is as if those stories demand to be told, and when one artist fails to ACT on behalf of that idea, "nature" finds a way. In the book, Gilbert discusses how she organically discovered that someone else on the other side of the world had nearly the exact same idea almost right after the original author had abandoned it. Essentially, someone else in the collective consciousness ended up following that same passion and ended up writing the book.

What ideas are calling YOU to tell them?

Are you willing to LISTEN? Or are you refusing the call? What would be possible if we all followed that passion inside us?

At our core, directors are storytellers. We are guardians of the TRUTH in the story and we must be masters of collaborating with artists who safeguard their own particular craft within the context of the greater whole.

This concept of "truth" is an interesting one too since there is a huge degree of subjectivity to whatever the "truth" might be. However, as director our job is to SEE the story before virtually everyone else – even if it is half-baked at first, and ultimately evolves into something very different – and then guide that story to completion.

Directing means different things with different disciplines, different things with different people, even how I work with various actors is different based on who they are.

That said, there are four general rules I use to consider my role as director:

1) Be in service to the story at all times.
2) Hire the "best" talent (on and off camera).
3) Be whoever I need to be to make the maximum impact with the person/people I'm working with so that they can do their best work.

4) Create the safe space for allowing the artisans and craftspeople I hire to do their best work. If I create the 'playground,' and encourage them to bring their A-game and experiment, take risks, and be bold, the results speak for themselves.

The last one can be rephrased as "get the hell out of the way." Yeah. Let's go with that one!

## IS DIRECTING MICRO-MANAGING?

Nope.

In fact, directors often speak WAY too much and end up confusing the situation.

Especially when it comes to on-camera talent, the spirit of *allowing* actions to take place and not micromanaging and micro-detailing every last breath makes a world of difference.

"Oh, but I want you to move here and then turn this 3/8 of a turn this way, cough a lil' then eek out the tiniest tear …"

*SHUT THE HELL UP!*

Do that and don't be surprised when everything is

robotic, or your actors just hate you. That's not magic! That's not actually evoking authentic performance, that's dictating. And the result? Stilted garbage.

I actually heard the director of *Whole Ten Yards* say once that when working with actors, "You don't get a dog, then bark yourself." GENIUS. It's really simple. Hire the best actors you can, and EVOKE. Don't try to do it for them and result-direct your actor all the way to the finish line. What you'll be left with is pure and utter garbage.

There is a difference between being a detail-oriented, thorough director that knows what they want vs. being a pain in the ass result-oriented director that gives feedback like "I need you to be more scared" or "Let's do it again, but sexier."

Create the most *authentic* story, whether it's through the acting, or with how the actors work with each other, the way that the camera moves, or with how the director's choice of lenses / shots that direct attention and tell the story, or whether it is how the music folds into the story to bring out that emotional experience.

## DIRECTING ATTENTION

At the core of it all, the director is directing the

ATTENTION of the audience. You're directing the eye to look at a certain part of the frame based on what is in focus or how the frame of the shot emphasizes or de-emphasizes the power of that person. Or, you're directing the attention to focus on the action or reaction in the editing room. Etc. etc. etc.

Every shot means something different and creates a different emotional experience. If you're doing one shot in one long, continuous take, this "one-shot wonder" type of mentality, you're deliberately choosing not to cut, which inherently *heightens the tension* of the moment – assuming what is available on screen is something worth watching and that we actually *care.*

If it's a suspenseful moment you're crafting, wouldn't it be valuable to speak the language of all of the different kind of disciplines? With sound design, if you choose to deliberately withhold sound, what does that mean for the bigger vision? How could that support the story? If it's a movie in space and all of a sudden it's this cacophony of sound in the hull of a space ship which explodes and then it goes abruptly silent because there's no sound in space, that's a deliberate choice. Depending on the context of the film, it could be extremely effective or it could seem like a mistake.

There are movies that are very effective when they use sound – or the absence of sound -- in a unique way to tell the story. *A QUIET PLACE* is a perfect example of how the absence of most sound can create a truly profound experience. In point of fact, the designers of that film actually use minimal sound and ambience to create the sonic contrast without resorting to a full void of sound. Conversely, *STAR WARS: THE FORCE AWAKENS,* was one of the first movies I ever experienced using the epic DOLBY ATMOS technology, which is stunningly immersive and captivating in its usage of new technology to enhance the movie-going experience. I had the opportunity to mix my short film *TRIGGER* in Dolby Atmos as well (the film is available on iTunes and Amazon, although sadly only available there in stereo).

## DIRECTOR / CONDUCTOR

As a young filmmaker, learning all of these disciplines, from acting, to camera work, to sound and music, to post-production editorial and color correction, enables you to maximize your effectiveness as a director. You must learn these various disciplines so you can communicate effectively with each of the different talents you bring on board your film. If you can't speak the language, you'll never be able to communicate your vision effectively in such a way where those talents can thrive and ultimately make your film come alive. This means it will require you to get your hands dirty and explore those various disciplines on short films and other projects before digging into a feature film.

This practice is essential. It is what will bring confidence to your craft.

When all of the disciplines are working together in concert, there is a synchronicity to the experience of making the movie and ultimately you will end up with a product greater than any one individual could create.

What lights me up about being a director is like being a conductor of the orchestra. From the creative side of things, the director is the one who is guiding the ship and working in harmony with the business side as well.

When I've seen my films projected on the silver screen up in front of audiences, seeing where people are in tears at the end of it, all of that makes the struggle of making films mean something so much more than just telling stories. If it brings some sort of an emotional catharsis, where someone either looks at their life a different way or they are able to heal in some capacity, that is something that is a very noble and honorable aspect of filmmaking and I think it's a necessary responsibility of filmmakers.

# *"With great power comes great responsibility."*

~*Benjamin Parker; SPIDERMAN*

So if filmmakers have that power, we need to yield it in a responsible way and really take that to heart.

We get to be rigorous with what we're saying and know that people are looking at it for deeper meaning and whether art is a reflection of society or vice versa, I think there's a clarity of context that needs to be set such that we're not perpetuating things that are holding the world back.

## WHEN IS A FILMMAKER READY?

When is somebody actually ready to shoot their first feature, or make their first project? How did I know that I was ready to make *CATALYST*?

I think you're ready when the film inside you can't wait to be told any longer. I knew that I had the story for *CATALYST* brewing inside and started toying with the idea almost half a decade before I ended up continuing the evolution of the story that ended up on screen.

Early on, I actually took a group of 12 actors and

threw them into the situation the movie explores, and it was very informative. A lot of the language and a lot of the premise was similar and it helped inform writing the first version of the script that was a full-length feature script, but the first version of the script was a damn mess. I tabled it. It simply wasn't ready to be brought to life.

I'm so glad I didn't shoot that version of the film. The kernel of the idea was there. Several years later, and after developing myself as a filmmaker in the commercial and promo world, and after testing various methods of production out with the spoken word "spinema" pieces I developed with my CATALYST colleague, actor/producer David Bianchi, things had transpired with seeing some of my other filmmaker friends do various other unique ways of making their movies that it also inspired me to think in a different way about the mechanism for how we could bring this movie to life in a fresh and unique way, while also creating maximum production value for minimal budget.

At the same time as I started noticing these developments, David Bianchi came to me and expressed the same degree of passion for bringing some sort of a project to life. He basically said: "We gotta do something." I responded, "I was literally about to call you to say the same thing. There's got to be a way to do something and I think CATALYST is the perfect project to make it happen in a unique way. What if we did it with seven actors instead of 12, and we threw people into the situation and did most of it in one night?"

We just started brainstorming on how it was actually POSSIBLE to make something when up until then it just felt impossible.

When I stopped telling myself I couldn't do it, finally I discovered all the ways I *could*.

There's science behind this. The *reticular activating system* is the reason why.

The *RAS* [reticular activating system] is essentially your brain's filter. Your brain is bombarded with roughly 11 million bits of data and the conscious mind is only really able to process 40-50 bits at a time, depending on who you ask. So the RAS helps you filter that by assessing what is "important" based on what you focus on most.

*SELF TALK => PROOF => BELIEF => SELF TALK => PROOF => BELIEF => SELF TALK => PROOF => BELIEF [and on and on]*

We end up living in this endless cycle so that we can be "right" about those beliefs.

SO you'll know when you're ready because that story within — I call it "the why" — that burning question, that burning desire will overwhelm you.

Is your passion, your will, your determination great enough that when your film demands that you reinvent yourself, you do it?

Are you willing to listen, are you willing to go after it, are you willing to do whatever it takes?

When you're ready to declare no matter what it takes, "I'm gonna get that film on screen." That's when you're ready to make the movie.

"I want to make a movie" is not enough.

I had that intention for half a decade.

I also had a lot of ego conversations that were speed bumps on my journey to finding the path to making it happen. All my attachments to "how it looks" were big obstacles that I needed to break through for that other one. The scarcity, the attachments to how it looks, and that need to be right as well.

It's not enough to simply say you want to make a feature if you haven't also simultaneously developed your sense of integrity. If you haven't already developed all of those other core elements of what we're about to discuss in the later chapters, it's not enough.

Yeah, you might go and try to make your film, and you might go actually make one, but is it going to get anywhere? How is it received? Have you done everything you can to secure the best distribution deal? How do you respond if it isn't received with critical and public acclaim? If you're not equipped with the best emotional intelligence strategies, one subpar review could send you into a tailspin and shatter hopes for a bright career.

There's so much "noise" out there right now with movies that are just movies that don't resonate deeply or that aren't perennial sellers or that aren't actually making the impact that the filmmaker had dreamt of.

You have to be willing to put the sweat equity in even when, and especially when, it gets difficult. You have to be willing to make the sacrifices and choose to withhold on temporary pleasures and conveniences for the sake of your creation.

At the end of the day, it's an experience. I think it's a feeling.

This is why I coach my students in the online course version of *DIRECTING YOUR DEBUT* (www.directingyourdebut.com) about knowing and being clear that if you're in this business for the fame, you're making a mistake.

Early on, I used to listen to directors' commentaries on every movie I could get my hands on and I specifically remember Michael Bay mentioning on one of his DVDs (I don't remember which one so I'm paraphrasing here), "This is just not a glamorous business. The business itself, not glamorous. It's war. Making movies is like war."

The dude is right. Making movies can get messy. There's a lot of politics involved. There's a lot of drama involved. You've got to be willing to continually reinvent yourself, your approach, and you've got to be willing to do whatever it takes to get that thing across the finish line, which means it's going to be work.

A lot of people expect someone else to do the work for them. That gets you nowhere.

Choose NOW. This is your chance to start addressing that internal conversation head on. Be willing to take your life head on.

That starts NOW. And only YOU can choose it.


## WHAT GIVES YOU THE RIGHT?

As a filmmaker, who gave you permission?

I don't think it matters. The idea that I have is not mine. It comes from something else. It's a muse.

Look at any of these books: *Big Magic*, *Catching the Big Fish* by David Lynch, the *War of Art* by Stephen Pressfield. That story you're being called to tell is coming from collective consciousness, so it's really not about me. And yet, it's all about "me owning my responsibility" in bringing that to life. It's not egoic at all.

If, however, I trust that I can be the vehicle for that vision to come to life, and trusting the skillset that I have to interpret that and bring it to life in a way that only my contribution can, then and only then, can that vision manifest.

## *"Direct the film that requires YOU to make it"*

~Christopher Nolan, Director

If you were to ask five different directors to interpret and execute on a particular story, you would be handed five *completely* unique and individual *interpretations*.

There's a creative ownership around it. And I don't mean ownership in the sort of legalese way of looking at it. It is more of a responsibility to tell that story and the artist who breathes life into that story shares a piece of his/her own unique voice.

For instance, I know that my short film *TRIGGER* saved lives around the world because of the stand that it is for LQBT lives and the cathartic experience the film can have on the viewer. In the same way, my feature film debut *CATALYST*, when it's released, will have an impact on people from a totally different context. I knew that both *TRIGGER* and *CATALYST* are stories that need to be told because the idea itself kept showing up for me – in my mind and on my heart – and I was willing to listen to that inner calling.

If I hadn't been willing to listen to that inner calling, then those films would have been left unmade. Or I would've been willing to more or less sabotage the idea "for commercial purposes" and make it more where everybody just kills each other and it's about making the next double digit iteration of *SAW*.

Instead, to be willing to come from a place of honoring the integrity of the story and being willing to redesign it as needed but not selling out on that initial vision, is the ultimate test of a director.

First time directors are called to declare a vision that is so bold that it's truthful and authentic and raw and unique. It is truly the story that only you are qualified to tell.

I was willing to listen to the voice inside me that said, "Make an online course." Because I made that online course, my students are making movies and other unique video content that are already impacting the world. They are following their passions. They are feeling more and more alive everyday. That wouldn't have happened otherwise.

It took being *willing to listen* first. The voice inside me says, "Write this book." I'm writing the book. There was a clarity of *knowing* that *felt right.* It felt like a win-win-win. There's really no way to describe the sensation of that inner knowing. If I were to try and put words on it, the closest thing would be that it almost engulfs my whole body.

It's kinda like the Marie Kondo method. When something "sparks joy" with me I know there's something to pursue there.

Those are the moments when I *feel* deeply enough that "this is something that really gets to happen." It isn't some shallow thought drifting in and out of my head. It is a deep, inner knowing. A truth.

After I started the process of writing this book, and given I've been developing this open channel to my inner authority, I started feeling: "Okay, there's another thing that I want to do called *MINDF\*CKED* that's on its way." Call it a sequel to this book/course series. If you're interested in where that's heading, check us out at www.mindfcked.com to get some free content when you sign up for the interest list now and add me on Instagram @chrisfolkens to keep the conversation going. As it evolves, you'll be the first to know!

When I say yes to these ideas, and I talk about it and I am held accountable to that, things start to happen. That connection grows stronger. When I don't just hold those ideas inside or deny them, but instead cultivate them and give them the time to percolate into what they're meant to be, that is the space where magic can happen.

I've seen that happen my whole life, where instead of following that voice within, I would watch people around me shut that voice down – both in me, and in themselves. I saw the prices all those people were paying.

Like a parent telling their child "you're not good enough" we walk around treating our intuition like that little child. Now, because we create more of what we focus on in our lives, we end up pouring our life force energy into believing that our intuition means jack sh\*t.

How's that working for us?

Following that voice, however, only continues to strengthen that connection. My early short film *DIVERSION* was just like that. *TRIGGER* and *CATALYST* have grown stronger and stronger in that awareness.

I could clearly see it in front of me that I need to follow this voice. Well, I don't *need to*.

But if not me, then who?

If not now, then when?

There's a saying: "Pain demands to be felt." Well, stories demand to be told. Right?

It is my sincere hope that those of you reading this book will be activated in such a way that you start listening to that authentic voice within. Scream at the top of your lungs (through whatever social media you have OR with whatever friends you have around you) that you are fully committed to following your passion. That you are committed to the #DirectingYourDebut challenge.

You're ready.
You're willing.
You're able.
You're COMMITTED.

If this lights you up and gets you following your

voice, tell another filmmaker friend close to you to buy this book and spread the word about it because the more people around you learning these mindset hacks, and standing for you to LIVE them, the more you will ANCHOR THIS CHANGE in your life.

It is one thing to intellectually "get" something. It is another thing entirely to LIVE your transformation. The accountability you will experience by sharing your commitment with the world, and activating the support systems around you, the more you set yourself up for success.

If you want to take that commitment to the next level, joining the *DIRECTING YOUR DEBUT: Online Course & Mastermind Group* may be right for you. But first, the basics. We must have a foundation to start with.

Whether it's a short film that's going to change the world or it's a feature film or a documentary or whatever else you're called to create, you owe it to yourself and to the world around you and to the people that look to you for guidance to say, "Are you following your dreams?" You owe it to yourself and to the world around you to find the means to reinvent yourself to create those works of art and get the support system around you to be able to make that actually happen. Get the coaching necessary to show you your blind spots and get crystal clear on what stops you from getting your vision on screen.

I've worked with plenty of people through the years that would rather be comfortable than actually follow their dreams. There are people out there who SAY they want to be a director (or always WANTED to be a director) but who take zero action toward that vision.

What is the message those people are sending to their children? Yeah, they got their quality time in, but now their children may give up on their dreams too because they were taught from a young age that life is always about an *either / or* conversation. The *win / lose* zero sum formula of life.

If you'd rather play in your comfort zone than take risks, put the book down now. Go find a "safe job" that keeps you stuck in a box.

If, however, you'd rather live on the skinny branches, be bold and follow your calling – even if you might fail – then you're in the right place.

If you're willing to challenge your internal roadblocks that keep you stuck – then you're in the right place.

If you are willing to believe that you CAN live that

dream you always had for your life, AWESOME. We've got somewhere to start. Your willingness to believe that you CAN is 100% the first step.

You're ready.

## ACTION STEP:

*Post to INSTAGRAM and/or TWITTER, then ADD #DirectingYourDebut & TAG me @chrisfolkens then either in your story video post or in the comments of the picture describe:*

*Did you give up on your vision for you life?*

*What became more important?*

*What will be possible when you break through your limitations?*

# 2 ROADBLOCKS TO THE DREAM

We've all heard "you are your own worst enemy" but how often do we actually take account of all the ways that is 100% the truth?

Stephen Pressfield, in *THE WAR OF ART,* talks about how what stands in the way of you living the "un-lived life" within you, all your potential, all your dreams, is this pesky thing called "RESISTANCE".

In a nutshell, "RESISTANCE" is all the ways we resist and avoid what our true calling is on this planet.

## WHAT STOPS YOU?

There are some "usual suspects" that stop *all* of us from creating the lives we dream of living. The major roadblocks almost always revolve around seven main "internal roadblocks":

-   fear of failure/success

-   fear of rejection

-   fear of judgment

-   need to look good / be liked

-   worthiness (not being enough)

-   scarcity (time/money)

-   fear of being uncomfortable (playing small)

Let's look at these one by one, shall we?

## FEAR OF FAILURE / SUCCESS

What's the worst that could happen you say? How about I fall flat on my ASS in front of millions of people? Both literally and figuratively...that would totally suck.

Well. Apply that to filmmaking and it is pretty clear

why people avoid putting themselves in "harm's way" by risking it all for fear that they may actually "fail" at creating something valuable.

How about shifting our interpretation of what is "valuable"? What if even the potential for failure is actually a good thing? What if even if we fail at landing with an audience in SOME capacity, that becomes a CLUE for how to re-invent ourselves and close that gap the next time around?

Then, ladies and gentlemen, failure doesn't exist. You take the pain out of failure by transmuting that "failure" into something where you actually want to "FAIL" as FAST AS YOU CAN! Why not get those damn failures under your belt early on so you it becomes a part of mastering your craft?

If you allow yourself to be DEFINED by your "failure" you'll never live to see your success. You will instead give in to that lie that the "failure" is bigger than you are.

The flipside – but equally as limiting here – is the fear of success! What you're scared about with failing magnifies if/when you actually DO become a success and the threat of falling from that height petrifies you.

Guess what? This is real. It is part of the human

psyche. But it doesn't need to paralyze you any longer.

Read on…

## FEAR OF REJECTION

Closely tied to that fear of failure / success is its ugly sibling the fear of rejection!

Who doesn't love getting turned down and flat out rejected? I know I do… wait, what?

I kid around here, but really, getting rejected kinda blows. From early childhood we're all inundated with feelings of rejection. Getting older doesn't make that go away. If anything, we continue to live out of that fear that to be rejected means we're somehow "less than."

I felt rejected growing up for everything from my choice to be in the band, to my weight, to my hair cut, glasses, whatever. The list goes on.

Except –

All the things I got rejected for actually made me into the filmmaker I am today. All those things I got rejected for because some other self-righteous kids made fun of me, they're the ones coming to me asking to be in my movies.

Nuff. Said.

Like with the previous section of fear of failure / success, once again, fear of rejection comes down to PERCEPTION.

My first boss straight out of college at the world famous advertising agency, Leo Burnett in Chicago, always told me "perception is reality."

For the longest time I resisted that saying because I felt like it was skewed at making me "wrong." And I hated being "wrong."

Well. The genius behind that saying is incredibly profound when you look at it on every different level.

Our perceptions are affected by our reticular activating systems [RAS, remember that?]. Our filters affect our perception and create our world around us based on how we see the 11 million bits of data that are bombarding us.

Therefore, if we choose to SHIFT our filter, we can choose to view these beliefs in a manner that empowers us. Forwards us. Elevates us.

## FEAR OF JUDGMENT

Remember what I was saying about being made wrong and how much I hated that? Well the fear of judgment speaks right to the heart of this issue. We are conditioned from an early age to fear being made wrong.

As a child, your parents most likely made you wrong in some capacity and that's how they mold you. In a way, that's what Don Miguel Ruiz speaks about in his book *The Four Agreements* when he talks about the concept of "domestication."

At that early age, human beings are domesticated into a system of reward / punishment.

Good / bad.

Right / wrong.

We HATE being "wrong."

Now. There isn't anything necessarily "wrong" with that system of domestication. But… what doesn't work is choosing to either play naïve to that system or not embrace it, and ultimately work WITH it. The minute we can identify or recognize where our autopilot programming of sorts is coming from, that is the precise moment we can actually do something to change things.

By being PRESENT and acknowledging the fear, we can choose to recognize it for what it is: judgment is a reflection of the eye of the beholder and their own personal filter.

We can never choose what happens TO us but we ALWAYS have the power to choose how we RESPOND.

## NEED TO LOOK GOOD / BE LIKED

Oh, HERE's a great one. This should be immediately clear to anyone living in or around Los Angeles. As a guy who grew up in Chicago, moving to LA instantly felt like "woah, I better start working out."

But where does that come from? Once again, this fear of our own "image" in front of others and whether or not we look good is so engrained in our culture. We literally live in an "image-based" world.

We're constantly inundated with advertising that reinforces that message: "drive this car / drink this beer / take this trip (or fill in the _____) so that people will think you're COOL / HIGH-CLASS / RICH…. or whatever."

But what if it's all just bullsh*t?!?!

What if – and here's where it may get a little woo-woo for some of you – even the mere notion that we're "separate" in the first place is all an illusion?

We've all heard the phrase "we're all ONE" right? At our very core, we're ALL just energy and vibration. Right? Ask any quantum physicist and they'll give you the long answer but for now, that's enough. So if we're really all that energy stuff deep down anyway, then everything *other* that that is all the stuff of illusion anyway. Our bodies are literally re-made from the cellular level something like every seven years. Completely new.

The WHOLE point in saying all of this is to emphasize that you and me… and everyone in between… are SO much more than "what we look like" or "how we look" to others.

We are something much, much, more.

My invitation to you here is to embrace the divine *gift* that you are and realize that your *contribution* is what matters. It will take some time to master that contribution into a craft and you better be ready to weather that storm of failure, rejection, and looking "stupid" as you iron out the kinks on your journey to directing your debut – or applying this to ANY creative endeavor.

## WORTHINESS

Do you believe that you are worthy of being called the "director"? Do you believe that you are worthy of someone giving you money to actually bring YOUR vision to life? Do you believe that you are worthy of someone spending 90-120 minutes of their life devoted to living vicariously THROUGH YOUR CHARACTERS and experiencing that through YOUR creative execution such that they LIVE and BREATHE in those characters' shoes?

If you show up unworthy to a pitch meeting…

GAME OVER.

If you show up unworthy to an investor meeting…

GAME OVER.

If you show up unworthy in a meeting with cast…

GAME OVER.

You get the point. Basically every aspect of life, from relationships to finances to family life, is impacted by the degree to which you either live into your WORTH as a human being or you choose to see yourself as unworthy.

Why? Because once again, your reticular activating system is only ALLOWING you to continue to see the evidence that supports your consistent beliefs.

Well let me put it bluntly, whatever spiritual force caused you to start breathing on this planet when you were born into this world, enabled that because you had a purpose for being here.

Discovering that purpose is UP TO YOU.

Once you find that purpose, it is ON YOU to hone it, refine it, passionately pursue it, and CREATE meaning in it.

You will never do any of the above unless you believe that you are worth the air you breathe.

Or that you are worth the investment of others in you.

Or that your VOICE matters.

It all boils down to worthiness. Do you believe in your inherent worth as a human being? A storyteller? A filmmaker? A director? If not, that will give you a clear roadmap of where to start.

## SCARCITY

This is another one of my favorites. It also happens to be the one internal "conversation" I've struggled with the most throughout my life. This conversation, however, looks different today than it did growing up or even when I first started pursuing my dreams of being a filmmaker.

Scarcity, as it pertains to limiting beliefs and the internal roadblocks that hold us back, has everything to do with scarcity of both TIME and MONEY.

How many times have you used the phrase "I can't afford it" or "I don't have enough money to _____" and then proceeded to derail any hope of doing what you wanted / loved / were passionate about?

How many times have you said "I don't have the

time to _____" and then continued to be right about that conversation, instead of challenging yourself to look at what it would take from you to rise above your circumstances and make that time, to LIVE INTO a declaration from your vision for your life instead of being a victim to your circumstances?

Your wallet AND your calendar are a reflection of your true priorities. They represent feedback. Results.

Now again… I say all this to be interruptive, not to be abrasive. I must emphasize that this sort of honest, direct, interruptive feedback is what enables us to really pinpoint those conversations that are truly holding us back, and then break THROUGH them such that they never hold us back again in the same way.

If we do that, our relationship to these limiting beliefs will never be the same.

It is important to notice that I mentioned my relationship with this scarcity conversation has shifted through the years.

When I first started pursuing filmmaking I most certainly had the scarcity conversation surrounding money. I always claimed that "I have expensive tastes" and "there's no way we'll be able to make _____ movie for less than $50 million (I'm exaggerating here for the sake of example)."

It is all too easy to get caught in the trap of believing you never have the money to take action. Then you can continue to play small. Whatever you do, do not think outside the box…

…or at least that's what your FEAR is telling you.

## FEAR OF BEING UNCOMFORTABLE

How often have you chosen to stay "comfortable" instead of living consistently with your vision for your life?

It can show up, like hitting the snooze button instead of actively taking action toward the life you want or perhaps not putting yourself in the running for opportunities that might be a turning point for you for fear that you might need to speak publicly, or do something else that might cause you discomfort.

There's nothing comfortable about subjecting your vision, your ideas, your dreams, your storyboards, your dialogue, your _____ for other people. Whatever it is, you MUST develop your threshold for being comfortable being uncomfortable in order to be ready for the pressures and demands of filmmaking – or pursuing any creative endeavor.

## SUMMARY

The DIRECTING YOUR DEBUT process is about learning to use all of these fears as a guide. A roadmap. Not the obstacles they used to be. It is an opportunity to re-define what you're made of. It is an opportunity to work WITH the universe to call yourself to a higher level. It is an opportunity to rise up to who you innately are, instead of who your conditioning would have you believe you are.

## ACTION STEP:

*Post to INSTAGRAM and/or TWITTER, then ADD #DirectingYourDebut & TAG me @chrisfolkens then either in your story video post or in the comments of the picture describe:*

*What is the story you're being called to tell?*

*What fear is running your life and stopping you from taking action?*

*What will be possible when you break through your limitations?*

# 3 THE SECRET FORMULAS

Human beings love knowing there's a "secret" formula out there. Do we not? We love to believe that there is some magic wand that we can use to finally generate results. We buy programs that advertise they'll practically write our scripts or craft our characters for us.

In order to direct your debut film, you'll need to let go of the notion that some formula is going to do the work FOR you.

Hate to break it to you, but there aren't any shortcuts. Transformation in our lives takes work. It takes a commitment to facing the difficult, walled off, sensitive areas we like to protect in order to keep us safe.

The real work, the real formulas that DO work are the ones that work on YOU. Not the ones that attempt to make your film FOR you.

The real work is the work we do on ourselves. It exists in the domain of challenging our fixed and limiting beliefs in order to transcend our circumstances and create things we never thought were possible.

Anytime you're challenging an existing belief structure you're going to notice *resistance*. That resistance is what keeps you where you are. Break through that resistance and look at the things that hold you back and you will notice your world will shift around you.

We are conditioned at an early age to live one way. We experience pain, attempt to bandage that pain by creating a "story" around it to prevent us from living that pain over and over again. Then we master that story, living our lives so we can *be right* about those beliefs. In a nutshell, we're "MINDF*CKED" from an early age.

Break the cycle of those thought patterns and you *CHANGE YOUR LIFE.*

Period.

Again, this applies universally to ALL artists not just filmmakers!

We're conditioned to believe that there is a formula in life. We're taught at an early age that if we *have* that shiny _____ (toy / dress / beer / car / girlfriend) we will be able to *do* _____ (all the things in life that now become possible by having that thing) and then we will finally *be* _____ (fulfilled, joyful, happy, grateful, loving, etc).

That. Is. The. LIE.

The faster you let that sink in the faster you get to the 'secret' formula if there ever was one. The 'secret' formula is only a pseudo-secret because we believe this lie so heavily that we refuse to consider the possibility of another way.

Instead of believing the lie for one day, one week, one month, whatever it takes… try on another way of life for once. Try on living that formula *in reverse*. Try on living *from* gratitude, joy, love by *being* grateful, joyous, loving, compassionate, authentic, vulnerable, and giving.

Living from that platform, you will necessarily show up differently. You will take actions you never thought were possible. You will go after things you previously avoided that finally get you closer to living the life you always dreamed of. You will *attract, magnetize, and manifest* the people in your life that will support you in generating the life of your dreams.

The closest thing to a formula boils down to just that: THOUGHTS cause chemical reactions in our body that result in emotional responses => you "show up" and ACT differently based on what emotions are consistently showing up => those actions ultimately create the RESULTS you have in your life and ultimately determine whether you live a life where you're merely surviving or where you're thriving.

So again, if you haven't created the RESULT of directing your debut film, by nature of the definition here you can trace that back to your THOUGHTS.

In the most generic sense, here it is:

### THOUGHTS + ACTIONS = RESULTS

But because I've been so heavily inspired by the work of Don Miguel Ruiz (and his sons Don Miguel Ruiz Jr and Don Jose Ruiz) and the Toltec wisdom out there, for the purposes of your work here in what I'm calling the "MINDF*CKED" process, we will call thoughts the "DREAM."

The "actions" portion of that formula is where I'll put the creative power of what we bring to the table and label it "CREATE."

Finally, the "results" portion of that formula seems to really encompass both the proverbial "good" and "bad" results we create in our lives. But since the whole purpose of the MINDF*CKED brand is to support people in getting out of their own way, it seems only fitting to stand that we should be aiming toward that life where we "THRIVE."

So here it is…

The "MINDF*CKED: SECRET-ISH FORMULA FOR BEING A BADASS"…

Drumroll….

### *DREAM + CREATE = THRIVE*

What would a life where you're *thriving* look like? Do you even believe it is possible? Notice how easy it is to turn sour even after just reading how your thoughts are the foundation for the formula from which all results in our life originate.

So really… what would that life where you're thriving look like? How would it feel? What would have you jumping out of bed in the morning excited to take on the day?

I got news for you.  We also live in a world where

we fall in love with the "mechanism." People around us lose a ton of weight and what do we ask them? We ask "HOW did you do it?" That phrase is deceptive. To create results we lean into the formula:

### INTENTION + MECHANISM = RESULTS

However, because we romanticize the mechanism, we put such little emphasis on the intention and think that only one diet, or one way to make a movie, or one _____ is the solution to our problems. Then we freak out when that one doesn't work right away and we disengage. We shut down.

SPEED. BUMP.

The mechanism lives in the domain of "WHAT". This book STARTS with the "WHY". By relying on our autopilot response of starting with "WHAT TO DO" we set ourselves up for self-sabotage.

THAT, my friends, is why this book focuses predominantly on the WHY and the HOW. Vision, intention, and removing internal roadblocks and resistance is the name of the game in developing the creative life you desire.

When you get clear on your WHY behind making movies and really live in that vision for your life and for the world around you, the HOW will follow because you will begin to propel action instead of resist action in your life. You will attract opportunity instead of repel it. The WHAT aspect of creating results comes long after you're crystal clear on your why AND you've developed yourself into the kind of person that can actually achieve the mechanism.

So in short:

### WHY => HOW => WHAT => RESULTS

Want to break the cycle of being MINDF*CKED? Take the following strategies to heart. Take on your life like never before. Find a mentor (you got me). Get honest about what *really* holds you back.

In the following chapter, we'll be examining each of the distinctions of mindset mastery that will support you in starting to break through the roadblocks to the dream. This is meant to create conversation and bring that conversation into the world using social media. I want to hear FROM YOU how you're applying this in your life. How have you seen these strategies come to life in your own life?

## ACTION STEP:

*Post to INSTAGRAM and/or TWITTER, then ADD #DirectingYourDebut & TAG me @chrisfolkens then either in your story video post or in the comments of the picture describe:*

*What is at stake for you?*

*What is the story you're being called to tell?*

*What will be possible when you break through your limitations?*

# 4  MINDSET MASTERY

Now begins the process of re-writing the autopilot conversations that have you stuck. Limiting beliefs be gone!

When you change your PARADIGM – also known as your thought patterns, or mental model – you change your world. Our thoughts literally affect our entire life.

The following strategies will be the starting point to breaking through the internal obstacles to your filmmaking career. You must start with "the man in the mirror." This represents the most basic framework for understanding the mindset it will take to BE who you get to be, in order to DO what you must do, such that you create the RESULTS you intend to create and finally LIVE that dream of becoming a film director!

# DISTINCTION #1: RADICAL OWNERSHIP

To start off, one of the key distinctions of mindset mastery is to unabashedly, unequivocally, undeniably come to the recognition that our life situation – where we currently are in life – is the perfect result of what we've been truly committed to in our lives.

It is one of the toughest pills to swallow in truly owning that if we're unhappy with our current lot in life, we get to take a cold hard look at all the BELIEF SYSTEMS that led to the CHOICES / ACTIONS, which led to the LIFE SITUATION we're experiencing now.

Whatever conditions or circumstances we were born into – that which we have NO control over – what we DO have control over is our perception, our filter, our belief structure. It starts with being present to the source of the beliefs we were conditioned to adopt through the influential forces in our early lives.

From that point, we get to own the prices we've paid for living under that status quo. Again, this is not to say that all these belief structures are bad / wrong since that is only living out of a survival context of "good/ bad" or "right/wrong." Furthermore, I would add that at that point we can and should embrace EVERYTHING in our lives *AS IF WE CHOSE IT*. This is a suggestion from the brilliant philosopher Eckhart Tolle. This immediately shifts our energy from one of resistance to one of allowing.

We must rise above that to look at purely a conversation surrounding "effective / ineffective" at living the life we truly desire. If we look at our lives as if the sum total of our choices equals the position we're in, that is a far more empowering place to come from than merely giving away our personal power to outside influences and circumstances.

How many people do you know blame anything and anyone OTHER than themselves for their position in life?

"I'm not directing because no one's ever given me an opportunity..."

"I'm not directing because I'm a woman and they don't give opportunities to women..."

"I'm not following my passion in life because I don't have the time/money..."

"I'm not directing films because I have a family

now. Do you know how much time it takes to be a parent?"

I'm not making these up. These are all things I have personally heard from people I've coached or from various people in my life – who shall all remain nameless.

At a certain point you MUST be willing to say "F*CK THE EXCUSES" and adopt a "I'M GOING TO DO WHATEVER IT TAKES [ethically, of course]" mentality.

When I finally started owning 100% responsibility for the results in my life, I finally had the power to do something about it. I finally realized that the prices I was paying for giving away my personal power / choice in the matter, were eating away at my passion. When I stopped telling myself how "I can't because…" and instead started shifting the conversation to "well I say I want to direct, but instead of practicing my craft and building myself up to be the director that attracts the work I desire, I am currently deliberately choosing to 'play small' here by not taking committed action." Merely owning that shift in mindset enabled me to see the corrosive affects of the victim conversation that was running my life up until that point.

By practicing radical ownership, I stepped into a new possibility: a life worth living. I started CREATING.

A music video, then a spoken word short film, then a teaser trailer pitch for a project that never went anywhere but helped develop skills I would use many years later on my feature film *CATALYST*. The many small steps added up to become the foundation from which *CATALYST* became possible.

## DISTINCTION #2: POSSIBILITARIAN

As a coach, one of the most pervasive internal limiting conversations I've ever encountered is the question surrounding possibility. We tend to look at life through the filter we've been conditioned to believe from childhood AND which we continue to reinforce based on our habitual evidence gathering to reinforce that belief structure. Therefore, it becomes that much more dangerous when you believe that you are limited. You continue to seek and find evidence to support that belief instead of coming from a place of possibility.

What if, instead of saying "I can't," you instead shifted to a position of "what if it IS possible?" or "coming from a place of 100% is possible, 100% of the time, how COULD we shoot a movie in one day? (or whatever your challenge might be)"

How often are we derailed by what we PERCEIVE are obstacles, but when we merely shift our perspective,

EVERYTHING changes and suddenly the seas part and miracles happen?

Truthfully it probably happens way more than you'd think. Why? Because of our hardwired natural "impossibility" conversation. If we grew up telling ourselves "nah, I can't" then we MISS the evidence telling us "YES, YOU CAN."

Well let's start re-writing that conversation here and now. And yes, there's science behind this too. Just look up neuroplasticity! As Neuropsychologist Donald Hebb first spoke in 1949: "Neurons that fire together, wire together." Our beliefs and patterns are formed and reinforced until we challenge them. So here we go!

Let's start with a simple notion from stoicism, shall we? There is a saying attributed to Roman Emperor Marcus Aurelius: "The impediment to action advances action. What stands in the way becomes the way." The inspirational author Ryan Holliday breathes life into this and many other stoic principles in his books on the topic. I highly recommend them as a deep dive into those principals because many of them were very much a part of my own growth as well long before I ever read his books, but he does a phenomenal job of bringing those concepts to life which is outside the scope of this book.

That said, the principal of choosing to view

whatever obstacle lies in front of you as an opportunity is worth its weight in gold. This is something that can literally change your entire life when you start to challenge your FIXED belief in impossibility with the GROWTH-DRIVEN belief in the possibility that the solution will present itself when you put your mind to the task and combine it with burning desire and unshakeable faith.

## DISTINCTION #3: HAVE WHAT YOU HAVE

One of the beautiful little turning points in my own breakthroughs that led to me diving head first into directing CATALYST, long before I knew how it would be possible, was I received a little pebble inscribed with the words "You have all the money you need, to do that which is yours to do."

For whatever its worth, those simple words caused me to take the leap of faith and put my own money on the line to start the production and get us through the first day of principal photography. Given the unorthodox and totally non-traditional mode of making a movie by a "first time feature" director, I wasn't willing to risk anyone else's money on the biggest gamble of my career. I wanted the proof of concept first before I went to other people for funds to carry us through to completion.

That single leap of faith was the greatest risk of the entire project. But the second I crossed that proverbial threshold, fully committed, and put my ass on the line, the universe fell in line and sent an army of people to support me in my journey through the years.

It is almost uncanny just how shifting my mindset to what is effectively a "gratitude" mindset – grateful for being enough, having enough – changed everything.

*"To have what you have never had, you have to do what you've never done." ~ Roy Bennett*

I love that quote because I think it is truly the next step once you start from a place of being grateful for what you have, and trusting that wherever you currently are is the PERFECT starting point for you.

YES, there might be room to grow… of course there is! You will grow INTO the director you need to become as you take that first step, but if you're not owning your inherent worth and value by being grateful for who you are, what you have, you will miss your shot. Why? You won't take that first step.

And… as Wayne Gretzky once said: *"You miss 100% of the shots you DON'T take."*

# DISTINCTION #4: SCARCITY / ABUNDANCE

What if, instead of saying "I don't have ___" we chose to re-invent ourselves by way of rising up to the occasion in order to change that conversation to "how CAN I afford it" (as Robert Kiyosaki says in his *Rich Dad, Poor Dad* book series). By shifting that internal conversation to "how CAN I afford it," we literally put our brains to work FOR us in finding a solution to our problems or circumstances instead of being controlled by them.

If you believe that you are a part of a universe driven by scarcity or lack, you will continue to discover and find evidence to prove you right. If, however, you choose to question that belief just enough to open yourself up to the possibility of seeing something NEW, then there is hope.

By merely questioning your initial fixed belief structure... the "I can't because..." or the "I can't afford it..." and instead standing for your ability to BOTH 1) be responsible AND 2) come from possibility rooted in the belief that we live in an abundant universe, we immediately crack open the window from which ANYTHING is possible. The conversation is elevated when you come from your vision for your life, vision for your family, vision for the world, and when you're crystal clear on what you are committed to creating.

Again, that is why addressing the belief structure (and the roadblocks it carries) is a critical first course of action. You cannot take the first step on creating your feature film until you first believe you CAN.

You will never believe you can until you believe you are ENOUGH and that your CONTRIBUTION matters.

Simultaneously, you will never fully believe you are enough until you also choose to believe you were born into an ABUNDANT universe, full of resources, energy, and people that are ready and waiting to support your vision. Why? Because you will not start to see the evidence until you shift your conversation!

It never fails to amaze me when I'm speaking to people about enrolling in my online course version for *DIRECTING YOUR DEBUT,* that NO SOONER do those prospective students all emphatically exclaim how committed they are to making their dreams a reality, and how bad they really want to learn, but then go right back to their old mentality of "I can't afford it" and "I don't have." Right back to scarcity. Lack. And truthfully, the online course is barely a fraction of the sort of money you'd need to source in order to make a freakin' movie.

Seriously. I said it before and I'll say it again: "How

you do anything is how you do everything!!" Why? Because it is all coming from the same set of limiting beliefs.

UNTIL.

YOU.

CHANGE.

YOUR.

BELIEFS!!!!

What is the ENERGY around your belief? Are you being a sad sack about it? Or are you coming from the place of "I may not currently have this money in my account but I WILL find a way, come hell or high water!"

It is that "I WILL FIND A WAY" mentality that changes everything. THAT is a belief in abundance. THAT is a belief in your self-worth. THAT is a belief that you have what it takes. And THAT is what I call being a badass. You show when you fully commit to yourself, to your vision, to your BELIEF that you are not f*cking around. You are ready, willing, and able to bust through any obstacle in your way.

# DISTINCTION #5: RE-DESIGN

I cannot tell you how many times my films have gone through this process of RE-DESIGN. If you're truly willing to put yourself out on the skinny branches of life and risk being vulnerable by sharing your ideas, your vision, your talent with the world....

"THE ONLY CONSTANT IS CHANGE."

Chris Rossiter, the first executive producer I worked with straight out of college when I first started producing commercials at Leo Burnett, used to always tell me that quote. I wish I would've gotten my head out of my own ass long enough to listen to the wisdom in those words. Producing commercials was a nonstop evolution. Why? Because the CREATIVE PROCESS IS A NONSTOP EVOLUTION. It is a push and pull of impulses (and in some cases politics) that lead to an end result.

The longer I spent resisting it and avoiding the wisdom in those words, the worse it got.

My short film *TRIGGER* went through an entire overhaul during the post-production process on that film. What started off as a 14-minute problematic short film became a tight 10-minute emotionally cathartic short film that REQUIRED me to throw out the initial version once it was "done" and re-design it from the ground up.

I share both versions with my students in the online course version of *DIRECTING YOUR DEBUT* because I think that alone is a masterclass in surrendering to the creative process.

If the vision you declare is so bold that it requires you to re-design along the way, I believe the "creative muse," as Stephen Pressfield calls it, speaks louder and louder along the way.

That inner voice will call to you when you least expect it, provided 1.) you let go of your resistance to your own intuition (as illustrated when you resist your worth, or stay stuck in scarcity conversations, etc) and 2.) you're willing to listen to that voice.

This very book you're reading now went through much the same process. I wrote the entire book, then scrapped the entire initial version of the book because I had a moment of clear intuition speak to me that the framework for the book wasn't what IT needed to be.

It is that moment, when you let the ART speak to you, that you know you're on the right track. When the art (your film, book, music, etc) tells you what it wants to be, and you've mastered the ability to listen to that inner muse, you take a gigantic step in the process of mastering your craft.

Now look, I'm not here to say I'm a master at film directing. I'm working on it. We all are. But what I do know is that the process of mastery takes commitment and perseverance and you're damn right that it takes the willingness to re-design, re-commit, re-invent.

The entire process of creating *CATALYST* has been a fluid process. We knew it would be like that going in, since it was a very unorthodox way of making a movie, but the process still never fails to amaze me.

Now that I'm in the post-production phase of the film, I'm discovering new and different strengths and weaknesses of the film that I will continue to address.

As Ryan Holliday writes in his profound book, *THE PERENNIAL SELLER*:

*"Our goal here is to make something that people rave about, that becomes part of their lives. The buried insights found in those other great works were not put there on the first pass. Work is unlikely to be layered if its written in a single stream of consciousness. No. Deep, complex work is built through a relentless, repetitive process of re-visitation."*

# DISTINCTION #6: BE THE CHANGE

Gandhi said, "Be the change you wish to see in the world." Well, I'm pretty sure that also applies to your filmmaking endeavors. We've already discussed the critical importance of coming from a place of personal responsibility and radical ownership. The notion of being the change inherently brings us back to BEING. Not just doing. This distinction invites us to remember that "being-ness" occurs on the level of THOUGHT.

By shifting your thought process about all of the above distinctions, and away from the roadblocks to the dream we discussed in previous chapters, you are standing as the source of transformation in the world around you.

But this part goes well beyond the other distinctions as well, by focusing your personal interactions with the people you have attracted to work on the film with you.

If you're noticing that you're finding lapses in integrity with your business partners, where in YOUR life are you slipping up on what you said you were going to accomplish? If you're noticing you're surrounded by a bunch of people who are adamantly committed to being RIGHT and abrasively bulldoze anything other than their own beliefs, where in YOUR life are you choosing to deliberately perpetuate that energy?

Energy doesn't lie. It also "gets all over" the people we surround ourselves with, especially on a film set. Use the energy of your crew as a perfect reflection of the energy you're bringing. The director is 100% the source of energy on set. If you're showing up like a sad sack sour puss victim, you're gonna have one hell of a terrible shoot.

Now, let me just say, I'm not saying all this to neuter the director and make them into a pushover. Have a voice. Own your voice. The director has certain responsibilities and prerogatives as part of their role as the creative arbiter on set. Someone must have the final say. If you seek to create films 'by committee," you'll never get very far.

Being the change also comes down to "clearing the space" with people you're holding resentment toward in your cast/crew – or even in your life in general – within a day or two at the latest. The longer you hold any sort of resentment, the longer that energy of resistance has you like a vice grip.

To explain the notion of "clearing the space," whenever you're feeling resentment toward someone for what could be considered something "they've done to you," you start by taking radical ownership of it. Clearing DOES NOT equal BLAMING.

I've seen far too many people pretend they're

clearing up the space with each other by just pointing blame. That never ends well.

Instead, what would it be like to say, "Hey _____, if you're open to discussing it, I would like to clear the space with you about when the other day when _____ happened. What I made up about **(fill in neutral event here)** was that _____.  That comes from a deep seated **(lack of trust / fear of unknown / daddy issues, anything that represents the source of the issue at hand with YOUR perception... NOT THEM).** What you can count on from me is _____. Can I count on you to work with me on _____"

I also highly recommend the book *NONVIOLENT COMMUNICATION* by Marshall Rosenberg for learning specific strategies in how to approach difficult situations and help to de-escalate situations like this.

The goal in clearing is to stand as source of the transformation of the relationship. You're owning your role in the interpretation YOU had that led to your resentment. It is NOT about the other person. However, when you show up this way, you're likely going to notice that the situation transforms into something where the REAL issue comes out or you're actually able to see the problem from the other person's perspective as well.

This sort of clearing forces people to look at their own perceptions and how events are NEUTRAL EVENTS by nature. Human beings are meaning-making machines!

Our pre-conceived notions about things/people/events necessarily shade our perceptions which impacts how we show up and necessarily impacts the results we create in our lives. The way people treat us is absolutely a reflection of our own perceptions for that very reason: how we act triggers other people's filters and perceptions which informs their actions, which then we perceive through our filters and which can continue to escalate.

So if we're not careful, the entire thing can spiral out of control. Hence, why clearing the space is so critical. By leaning into the "pain" or resistance and looking at the issue beneath the perceived issue, you are directly challenging the unhealthy pattern.

To be clear, this isn't at all intended to be 'victim shaming' in the slightest. It IS, however, intended to point to the fact that the ONLY thing we do have control over is our own perceptions. We have zero control over what happens TO us, merely the perception we have over how we choose to look at what IS happening, HAS happened, or what MIGHT happen in the future.

By shifting our perceptions we actually retain our personal power to choose.

# DISTINCTION #7: TRUST THE PROCESS

I love this phrase. I've heard it used in so many contexts it's crazy. I even use it as a tagline from the mysterious organization running the psychological trials in my film *CATALYST*. I find the phrase fascinating because I think it means different things in different phases of my life. Life is a process. Filmmaking is a process. The creative process is… well that one is obvious.

Think about it. If we're not trusting the process, we're resisting the process. If we're resisting the process, we're our actual own worst enemy.

This doesn't mean I'm saying you always need to go along with everything. No. Own your voice!!! AND, trust that sometimes the very thing that seems like it is going to derail you, or when that location falls through at the last minute and you're convinced you're f*cked, THAT is the time when you get to remember to TRUST THE PROCESS.

I also invite you to consider that the process of creating a feature film (or any film/creative project that involves a variety of people to be involved in order to bring it to fruition for that matter) is necessarily a process that must be trusted to unveil what that film (or creative project) wants to be. That is a scary proposition for someone who grew up as a self-proclaimed control-freak. Those of us who like to control things to the n'th degree – you know who you are – are no doubt suffering from the loss of the *magic* that comes from surrendering to the creative process.

If you're willing to listen to your inner muse, your intuition, universal intelligence, or any other name you want to call it, you will be in for a treat. Trusting that the art will reveal itself by the process of constantly chiseling away at anything that is not the masterpiece is a skill that must be desired, then mastered.

You cannot expect yourself to START with this form of mastery. You must actively work on your art to where that voice inside gets louder. This takes a willingness to explore. To experiment. To FAIL as fast as you can so you can pick yourself up and learn from those "failures." It takes a willingness to create, then release that work into the public eye so you can learn from how people RECEIVE your work – while simultaneously NOT taking their feedback personally.

If you go about your life taking feedback – from your actors, crew, execs, reps, audiences, coverage on scripts, etc. – personally, you will never get anywhere. When I say "taking things personally," what I mean is that you are choosing to view that feedback specifically as a PERSONAL ATTACK or as something that DEFINES WHO YOU ARE as a person.

Feedback is purely neutral information. Feedback on your art. Feedback on how you're showing up. Feedback on whether what you've created is LANDING with an audience or not.

I tend to create films that require an audience to actually do some work too, not just sit there and be entertained. I am inspired by the films of Christopher Nolan because some of his best films call for that same level of audience involvement.

The moments where you feel like you are being pulled around in a whirlwind, where the "process" is calling you to question who you are, what you really want, and why you're really creating your art.... Guess what? Those are a challenge from the universe when you're on the verge of something great. I like to think the universe/God/whatever you want to call it... is up there saying, "You're ready for your next evolution."

So...

...are you willing to listen?

## ACTION STEP:

*Post to INSTAGRAM and/or TWITTER, then ADD #DirectingYourDebut & TAG me @chrisfolkens then either in your story video post or in the comments of the picture describe:*

*Which of the seven distinctions do you struggle with and WHY?*

*What are you willing to create TODAY that will directly challenge that struggle and challenge the various roadblocks by implementing the distinction you read about in this chapter? It does NOT need to be film related.*

# 5 **MY DIRECTING PHILOSOPHY**

Now that we've 1) gotten clear that you're passionate about living the dream of being a director, and 2) we've started to look at the roadblocks to that dream, then 3) discussed distinctions of leadership to support you in breaking through those roadblocks and being a leader in your life instead of being led by your circumstances, I'd like to take this opportunity to share some specific philosophical perspectives on directing. This isn't meant to be an exhaustive list and it certainly isn't meant to suggest that there is a "right" way to direct.

I share these in hopes that it may support you in removing some of the fear surrounding the directing process and also give you some ideas of what you may want to focus on to round out your skillset.

## STORY IS KING

People will buy into your film based on how they're moved by what you're creating. This comes from telling stories that are primal. Stories that tap into something innately human.

There are entire books about the various archetypes of story you can choose to employ. In fact, Christopher Booker's THE SEVEN BASIC PLOTS outlines these in a very LONG read (or lengthy listen if you're choosing the audiobook version), but I actually learned these basic archetypes in my work creating advertising and marketing.

If "OVERCOMING THE MONSTER," "RAGS TO RICHES," "THE QUEST," "VOYAGE AND RETURN" "COMEDY" "TRAGEDY" and "REBIRTH" sound familiar, it's probably because you've seen these sorts of stories your entire life. They're everywhere.

Joseph Campbell wrote of the monomyth which is also called "the hero's journey" and if you think about life, this is how we transform our very own lives.

PHASE ONE: SEPARATION (from the world we

once knew – "the original world")

PHASE TWO: INITIATION (into a new way of life in the "world of the unknown")

PHASE THREE: RETURN (to the "original world" to transform the world)

These stories involves death of the old way of life and being born into something new. TV deals with these sorts of transformations in a "day in the life" scope whereas film tends to deal with much larger scope.

Stories move us. Stories can come alive. Stories sell. They do these things because they tap into our inherent humanity and cause us to live vicariously, to grow, to have a cathartic experience, and/or to truly expand our consciousness.

When you realize that the process of you creating your own film is precisely your own "hero's journey," you will be that much closer to breaking through what is holding you back. This very book is structured along the narrative of the hero's journey. You must leave the world you once knew (your stasis, your limiting beliefs) in order to transform your ways (adopt the distinctions of leadership, publicly declare what you're creating, etc in order to live your vision for your life) and then return to inspire the world around you.

Remember… story is king.

## CHOOSE A STORY THAT IGNITES PASSION

You must be PASSIONATE about the story you're setting out to tell. If you're not passionate about the story you're telling, that energy will infect your set and ultimately destroy the integrity of your film.

Let's face it, you're going to be spending an obscene amount of time bringing your vision to life. If you're not so in love with that story, you're selling out on your cast, your crew, your investors, and most notably YOURSELF.

If you're not going to bring your absolute best, GO HOME.

If you're going to half-ass your way through your film, just be a plumber. At least there will be job security.

Film demands you show up and show up big time. When you're truly passionate about the story you're telling that will be infectious. Your cast will get that. Your crew will get that. The audience will get that.

83

## TRUST YOUR INNER VOICE

I've talked before about being willing to listen to that inner intuition, that inner voice. There was a moment on set of *CATALYST* where I wanted to really crack one of my actors and I knew that the actor himself (and also the character) were pretty hard-edged, masculine guys with a genuine desire for human connection.

We were getting to a pivotal scene in the film for this actor and although the scripted scene was powerful on its own, I felt like there was something missing when we saw it unfolding on the day (during production).

I felt compelled to create an added interaction that was not in the script and one in which the principal cast member would be surprised by – so much so that I knew it would break him down to that raw humanity I knew 1) he was capable of tapping into, and 2.) would be perfect for the scene because that was where the character wanted to go.

I kept it a secret. Went to his scene partner and told him to "touch his face, as a father would his son… a son he's proud of. You see the diamond in him. The diamond he's forgotten."

The moment was beautiful.

I'm so grateful I chose actors that trust me, and trust each other. The more I trusted my inner voice and intuition, the more they opened up and surrendered to the moment as well.

Directing is so much about cause and effect. By trusting my inner intuition, it led me to what I inherently knew would cause the moment I was looking for without resorting to the cardinal sin of directing: result-oriented directions like "be sad" or "be distraught."

## GET TO KNOW YOUR ACTORS AS PEOPLE

When I first started working in this business, I was intimidated by celebrities. I was terrified.

Guess what? THEY'RE PEOPLE. They breathe the same way you do. They bleed the same way you do. They have hopes and dreams, the same way you do. They love and are loved, the same way you do.

We often get lost in our FEARS when talking with people who may intimidate us because we start getting SELF-conscious. We're measuring, comparing, judging. We're coming from a place of lack. We're coming from a place of unworthiness.

Sound familiar? Perhaps like all those "roadblocks to the dream" we discussed in chapter 2?

SHOCKING!!!

Well here is a perfect opportunity to bust through that sh*t. It's time you recognize that your inherent worth as a human being is precisely the same as literally every other human being on this planet. We just sometimes struggle with recognizing that.

When I coach people, I invite them to really anchor to a "platform" or a "homebase" of sorts, which is essentially an affirmation. The purpose of this is to affirm the core of your being.

For instance, I know that I am: 1) creative, 2) courageous, 3) compassionate, 4) inspirational, 5) faithful.

I am many more things, of course, but at my core I know these five words illustrate a snapshot of who I am. Affirmations are often written from the context of "closing the gap" and supporting the transformation of thought processes by standing in the result one is intending to bring about. For instance, if you were to struggle with confidence, you might use the affirmation "I am a confident man" until you believe it to be true. That would represent a sort of "closing the gap" mentality.

What I'm inviting you to create in your platform, however, is to assert in 4-5 words who you KNOW you truly are deep down and what you've never really questioned. This is the first step.

By standing in that platform, I can *relate* to most people because I know each talent – cast or crew – matches one of those five words in some capacity. This is a way of starting with that sense of shared humanity and instantly breaks the barrier of nervousness. By focusing on THAT, it immediately shifts perspective away from whatever nervousness or SELF-focused perspective might otherwise have us thinking. Why? Because we're focused OUT.

When in doubt? Focus OUT.

## SOME PEOPLE WILL HATE YOUR FILM

Yep.

This one's simple.

Deal with it 😄

## NO REALLY. SOME PEOPLE WILL REALLY HATE YOUR FILM

I couldn't resist on that last one. So yes. Art is subjective and truthfully if you're trying to make a film that covers EVERYONE, you're not going to make something that carries an authentic message, and it'll probably end up being liked by NO ONE – or just, no one will end up seeing it.

Think about it. Remember those people that "tried to be liked" by everyone in high school? How'd that work out for them?

People have opinions. Strong ones.

If people can hate *STAR WARS*, that alone should tell you something. Even hardcore *STAR WARS* fans sometimes hate on the most recent *STAR WARS* films as you've no doubt heard – they're often very loud with their troll-like disdain. I happen to like the most recent additions to the *STAR WARS* lineup since Disney took the reins from Lucasfilm because I think they've done an incredible job of crafting these films – for the most part – and I love going along for the ride!

Now, what did I say about taking things personally?

DON'T DO IT!!

At the end of the day, people's reaction to your film is BOTH 1) a reflection of their own filter for how they view the world/themselves/etc, and 2) how your film either worked/didn't work in their mind. If at the end of the day you view that feedback as "it landed for them" or "it didn't land for them," there's a lesson in that. You can do something with that. It doesn't need to derail you.

I also tend to think that some people are just flat out attached to what they think a movie SHOULD be and therefore they miss what it IS.

I often wonder just how that hyper-attachment affects those people in their day-to-day lives. How you do anything is how you do everything so I can guarantee you that those people show up that way everywhere else and they are undoubtedly paying prices for it. What would life be like if you opened up and let go of that attachment?

## DRILL DOWN

Before you get lost in the profound scope of the task of directing, just break it down. When you sit down to put together a 5,000 piece puzzle how do you do it?

Piece. By. Piece.

What makes you think a film would be any different? So often, we get lost in the chaos thinking "oh man I don't know where to start!"

Just widen your scope. Realize that every film is a

collection of ACTS (typically three)…

Those acts are made up of SEQUENCES…

Those sequences are made up of SCENES….

Those scenes are made up of SHOTS…

Those shots are made up of TAKES on the day.

These are the building blocks. Don't freak out about the whole movie when the further down that list you get, the more and more control you have over OPTIONS.

I like to think of making a film like a wonderful five-course dinner. There's an overall flow to that dinner that is pretty standard. There's a flow to it [appetizers before entrees and followed by a delicious dessert]. No one questions that flow. In film, this is like the three act structure!

Within that flow there are sequences of 2-3 appetizers, then possibly 1-2 entrees, followed by dessert.

Within those sequences there are individual dishes. In film, this would be the scenes that make up each sequence.

Within each dish of this delectable dinner, there are

a variety of ingredients that came together to make that delicious flavor you're experiencing and which the chef landed on as the perfect combination to create the desired result in YOU.

Before that dish was ever presented, that chef went about trying so many options and really learning and growing to be the best that they could be. All that prep work represents each and every "take" you do on set AND all this prep work you are creating to get you ready for that experience.

All of it is part of the greater whole.

## FILM CAN BE ANYTHING

I had the opportunity to hear Christopher Nolan speak in Los Angeles once when he was touring with the glorious film print he helped champion for *2001: A Space Odyssey.*

During that speech, Nolan mentioned that one of the things he loved about *2001: A Space Odyssey* was that it was a reminder to him that "film can be anything."

That really moved me. It inspired me to be that much more authentic in a very raw and real way to the stories I'm being called to tell without being attached to films looking or being a certain way.

Now. It goes without saying that it is essential to learn and know the rules before breaking them so that they are informed choices. However, rules are not meant to be handcuffs.

## INDENTIFY, ATTRACT, ATTACH, MANAGE

Chris Rossiter, my first executive producer, also used to define agency producing using the above four words as a job description.

Start by IDENTIFYING the best talent…

ATTRACT them to your project…

ATTACH them to your project…

Then MANAGE the process.

While these words most definitely describe producing, there is also a lot of overlap with the indie film directing world and I highly encourage filmmakers to become masters and this process as well. You will likely need to have your hand in the producing pot to a degree along the way!

## WHEN/HOW TO REHEARSE

Rehearsing scenes never really looks the same way for me. Sometimes we get time to sit down and really workshop and explore. Sometimes we get very little time. But there should always be SOME time.

You can literally rehearse a scene using nothing but speaking the subtext to each other.

You can literally rehearse a scene completely flat (no inflection).

While I'm rehearsing I like to keep forwarding the momentum using the "yes, and…" mentality. This keeps the actors open and exploring as opposed to hitting a wall of resistance from rejecting any of that exploration.

I like to think of the rehearsal as the playground. We get to explore intentions, tactics, come up with a short-hand, and I ultimately get to learn what is working and not working about the scene, writing, work methods, and really feel out what will evoke the best in my actors.

## VISUALIZE THE STORY

Close your eyes. Experience your movie, from the first frame. What does it FEEL like? How does it come alive for you?

Back when I was first declaring that *CATALYST* would become a reality, and subsequently in between each of the multiple phases of production, I would go start location scouting and literally stand in the location I felt would bring that film to life.

I did the same thing with *DIVERSION,* my short film from 2010.

Getting into a physical space that allows me to visualize the actors moving around, even simulating camera moves on my iPhone, listening to film scores in my earbuds in the moment, all create the perfect scenario for me to live it before it comes to life.

This is incredibly motivating. Not only does that process motivate the sh*t out of me to go actually make it happen, but it becomes like a drug. The more exciting that gets, the more you really want to live that day in real life.

## BEWARE OF ATTACHMENT TO OUTCOMES

If you are just as attached to what things SHOULD look like, you will 100% miss the magic that is possible right in front of your eyes.

If, however, you come from a space of exploration, intrigue, curiosity, you will find a wealth of beautiful possibilities and the art will start to speak to you.

Have an opinion, but be open to being enrolled in the value of a different opinion.

## TELL THE STORY VISUALLY

This is a tricky one, especially for first time directors that likely are dealing with what could end up being a very "talky" movie.

Let's face it. When you're dealing with minimal budgets, the default is to lean into doing the "it's just two people in a room" type of film. Or whatever. Believe me, I've done that type of film. It's called *TRIGGER*. But even when you're dealing with what is ON PAPER a "simple" concept, you can still find a way to tell the story visually and push the envelope of what such a "simple" concept can be.

Can you use your opening and closing shots to show the transformation of your lead character?

Can you use the kinetic energy of your camera work to direct the attention of the audience and create a feeling?

Can you use the editing of your film to conjure up emotion in the audience?

Can you employ specific color palettes to support that emotional mood?

Can you use various lens choices to alter the perception of the story and further create that emotion?

The answer to all of these is a resounding YES. Overall, HOW can you use the art direction to tell the story? Some people like to use the term "cinematography" for what is really "art direction" in the design of the shots, so be careful not to confuse the two. I tend to view "art direction" as directing the attention by way of shot and lens choice, movement, kinetic energy, in such a way that creates the overall tone of the film.

As director, it is your job to guide those departments. However, guiding those departments doesn't mean dictating. If you hire the best talent and evoke their greatness, they will bring their A-game and elevate the entire film. Being a director is NOT about wearing all the hats – although sometimes you may need to wear a lot more than just the director hat on your early films.

I can only cover so much about this topic in a book format. Not only is that not the focus of the book.

However, in my online course I work to bring this to life for my students. This is the kind of thing that needs to be practiced and perfected: both spotting it AND implementing it.

## LEARN EMOTIONAL INTELLIGENCE

IQ is NOT the deciding factor on success. As Maya Angelou said, *"People will forget what you said. People will forget what you did. But people will never forget how you made them feel."*

Emotional intelligence, or "EQ," was first introduced by Drs. Travis Bradbury and Jean Greaves and deals with essentially four different areas of focus:

1.) Self-awareness (mindfulness and perceiving your emotions, and I would add being willing to uncover the true *source* of your emotions *a.k.a.* the personal "issue beneath the issue")

2.) Self-management (the ability to re-direct and channel your energy into something that forwards and is constructive for all around instead of adding to toxic energy, etc)

3.) Social-Awareness (being present to the emotions of others and perceiving the underlying causes of whatever surface issues might present themselves)

4.) Relationship-management (like self-management, this is the ability to use your perceptions of others and yourself to lead your team through conflict and/or to manage people effectively.

I've studied various aspects of Emotional Intelligence and leadership studies since college and I can honestly say, this work is some of the most rewarding self-development I've ever done. It also happens to be directly related with film directing. Studying people and how they work will only make you a better leader, better storyteller, better director, better friend, better family member...

You get the point.

Studying personality styles and even biotypes of various people has impacted how I read people and work with people based on what I know THEY are listening for. This is material I do a much deeper dive into in the online course version of *DIRECTING YOUR DEBUT,* especially as it specifically relates to film. The interactivity that an online course allows for is precisely the sort of format to EXPERIENCE what I'm talking about, not just read about. The whole point here is that none of this book will mean anything to you unless you actually translate that from the "concept" phase to the "experience" of living it.

Investing in yourself and your ability to work with people will only ever lead to more success and more flexibility in your career path. These are fundamental LIFE skills and for some unknown reason they don't actually teach THIS in school...

Yet.

## TRUST YOUR COLLABORATORS

If you're able to actually ditch the unhealthy version of your ego by learning and practicing emotional intelligence and mindfulness, you will actually learn to evoke and celebrate the contributions of your crew members instead of shutting people down.

Trusting your collaborators does NOT mean listening to, or agreeing with, everything they say. On the other hand, you do not want to work with / hire sycophants either – people that just agree with everything you say or flatter you. I think the perfect blend is bringing on people who respect each other but still have a unique voice and opinion that you know will add a certain voice to your film.

IF you've chosen quality, hard-working, integrity-driven people to work with you, then trust that their contribution comes from a place of love for the project, for the relationship you've fostered, and for the commitment to rising through hardship and ushering a project through the chaos to success.

## WHEN THE SH*T HITS THE FAN

When faced with the tough choices, what does your character CHOOSE?

All the great screenwriting teachers, most notably Syd Field in the book *SCREENPLAY*, talk about how character is revealed through the choices that character makes along the way.

There's a video of Matt Stone & Trey Parker, the creators of *SOUTH PARK,* speaking to NY Film Academy classes and sharing their quick trick to tell whether an outline is working or not.

Trey shares that if you look at your outline and "if the words 'and then' belong between those beats you're f*cked."

He goes on that "what SHOULD be between those beats are the words 'therefore' or 'but'."

What this does is essentially support you in

ensuring that you don't end up with what could be aptly called, according to author and speaker DMA (a.k.a. Donna Michelle Anderson) a "series of related events" (they're all in the same film and have some common denominators).

The PLOT should be in a "causal" relationship. In terms of plot point "speak," the inciting incident may be one of those rare occurrences where something happens TO the characters as opposed to their choices guiding the plot.

I will also add that this section should be used to also comment on how YOUR character is revealed through YOUR choices when the proverbial "sh*t hits the fan" on set or in at whatever moments throughout your film production.

## EMBRACE EVERYTHING

One strategy to lean on when faced with difficult situations on set is to do as the modern day spiritual teacher Eckhart Tolle says, which is to "embrace everything as if you chose it."

Think about it. What would that SHIFT in you, if you chose to employ that sort of mentality when faced with things that seem out of your control?

This doesn't mean to be literal. But if you operate from the platform of radical ownership, you will find this easier.

If you actually embrace everything, you stand a chance to re-direct that energy into something that is forwarding for you and your team.

There were some very trying moments throughout creating *CATALYST* where I found myself leaning on this mindset. When faced with crew member disagreements and/or tensions between different people that both meant well, but who were flat out *not listening to each other*, it took patience and persistence while constantly rooting my own perspective in gratitude for their unique gifts and talents UNTIL they both discovered it themselves. As I continued to practice gratitude, I watched their energy shift.

Remember, as director, you truly do stand as source for the energy in and around your set. While that may not be "fact," I invite you to come from the position that "what if that were true? What would be possible if I come from a place of it being true while dealing with my cast/crew? How might that shift the troubling energy I'm experiencing?"

## EMOTIONAL CORE ADJUSTMENTS

Never. Ever. EVER think your film is going to come out "as scripted" if you intend for it to be the best version of your film. If you remember back to the discussion of "re-invention," you should be crystal clear that to maximize the creative process, it demands that you be open to what the film wants to be.

Get ruthless with the film and be ready to "kill your darlings" while being clear on the story you're committed to telling in the most effective and emotionally compelling way.

## TRUST THE AUDIENCE & IGNORE THEM

I LOVE testing my films in front of audiences.

Actually, it sucks. But it's awesome.

Follow me on this...

Putting your baby up in front of an audience for them to pick it apart is a terrifying endeavor for any creative professional. That said, if you can develop thick enough skin to handle honest, direct, interruptive feedback on your baby, you may actually find that this feedback is instrumental in guiding you to listen to what the film wants to be after all.

There's no one RIGHT way to make a movie. Get over that sort of notion right now.

What the audience comes back to you with is a reflection of who they are, how they see the world, and what their expectations and attachments are. You are listening to their feedback as a sort of snapshot of what your potential audience might experience.

That said, wouldn't it make sense to target audience members that make up WHO YOU ACTUALLY WANT TO LOVE AND SUPPORT YOUR MOVIE?

Probably, yes.

If I show my contained-mystery-psychological-thriller *CATALYST* to an audience that hates this type of movie, or one that loves rom-coms or family films or who only watch hyper-Christian movies, how do you think it's going to go over?

However, I will say that, if you can hone in on the target audience, you want to become champions of your movie and listen to how they RECEIVE the film, you may just find some invaluable feedback that will guide you in crafting and re-crafting (hint hint, remember the concept of "re-design") until you arrive at a story that just clicks.

One of the reasons I created the *DIRECTING YOUR*

*DEBUT* online course was because I wanted to create a mastermind of filmmakers that 1) know their sh*t, and 2) that are not afraid to speak up and give honest, direct, interruptive feedback to each other in an effort to stand for their GROWTH.

Again, choosing to buy this book and read it does NOT mean you're going to go make your movie. You must be willing and ready to transform your vision into a reality by getting committed to taking this off the page and into your life. You get to turn this from merely a concept into the experience of living it.

# 6 **THE FIRST STEP**

Whatever you do, do NOT do "nothing."

You've come too far for that. What do your dreams actually mean to you? What does living this vision for your life actually mean? Are you willing to get inconvenient in order to achieve it? Are you willing to suspend temporary pleasures to invest in yourself? Are you willing to get uncomfortable and put your work out there for people to see and comment and judge?

What is this worth to you?

One thing is for sure, if you just take that "first step," the next step will start to become clear. Then the next. Then the next.

You don't need to do any of this alone. You got me. You have an entire support structure around you. While I believe the online course is an effective way of doing the "advanced version" of the work you're starting here, if you even utilize social media and start tagging each other with the hashtag #DirectingYourDebut on Instagram and Twitter, you'll find each other and will be able to have that common denominator of this work.

That is my dream. That is my vision. It is time you take the reins and choose the path that is right for you.

If you are interested in continuing on don't hesitate and reach out to me at chris@directingyourdebut.com or check out the FREE webinar at www.directingyourdebut.com on the main page.

I absolutely love hearing from students and/or people I've coached to learn that they got out of their own way, took control, and found a way to take that first step. I can't wait to see you get started and to hear your success story when your film is on that big (or small) screen!

# ABOUT THE AUTHOR

Christopher Folkens is an Emmy-nominated commercial director and repeat Telly Award winning music video director with over a decade of experience creating Hollywood caliber productions. Through the years, Folkens cracked the code on what it takes to actually BE the director it takes to overcome every obstacle and bring that debut film to completion with confidence and style. Drawing on his experience as a leadership and personal development coach for over seven years, Folkens helps students jump into their own filmmaking endeavors in the online course version of Directing Your Debut (www.directingyourdebut.com) and is currently completing production on his own feature film debut "CATALYST" (www.catalyst-the-movie.com).

Made in the USA
Columbia, SC
06 December 2020

26545565R00065